PRAISE FOR moon*dancing*

"I love the structure, and couldn't put it down once I started reading it. Bernadette's Moondancing proves to be the simplest, divinely effective self-guide to getting to know and learn how to manifest through the cycles of the moon yet! This program may take one from beginner to intermediate creative moon devotee within a few months' time. Surely, it is a guide to use time and time again—and with room for reflections, the learner is bound to discover some magic all on their own."

— **Michelle Quesada**, *Michelle Quesada Art, Mused and founder of The Mused Community/Creativity Challenges*

"Bernadette Rose Smith is a goddess who inspires, motivates, and personifies the very definition of a muse. The formula in this artists' path is like a gentle, spiritual love song to the reader. Leaving plenty of room to visualize, add notes, and pictures, the reader is free to capture their own unique dance. These practical, yet evolving interactive steps and clear direction, provide a purpose driven path, which unveils and catapults the reader toward their own divine potential. If what you are looking for is a way to launch a new adventure or release untapped talents, then this inspired work is definitely for you. Moondancing is a brilliant catalyst for all women who are looking for the incentive to be their own muse. You will not want to miss this rare experience of lessons learned, which can be passed down through generations of dancing souls still to arrive. Time to dance Lovies, our passionately creative muse is waiting on the dance floor!"

— **Kimberly Jones Sanford**, *Sassy Southern Diva – Writer*

"Moondancing by Bernadette Rose Smith is a must have for anyone on a path of self-discovery and reflection. I love the concept Bernadette has so aptly captured with the energy and cycles of the moon as you journey from start to finish. Each cycle's energy translating into practical steps of creating and manifesting your wants and desires to fruition. I know the law of attraction and manifestation process can seem woo-woo to many, but in her skilled wisdom of guiding you through the processes of each step with playfulness, creative exuberance, and authentic sharing of her own journey, you can feel her right there with you on your own journey. I loved how Bernadette brought the art of seeing life through different perspectives to the forefront in her own way, and in a way that I know will enrich my life so much more."

— **Di Riseborough**, *Intuitive Life Strategist, Author, Speaker and F-Word Specialist*

MORE PRAISE FOR **moon**dancing

"Like many, I was creative, perhaps even artistic, as a young person, but this was not celebrated with outrageous enthusiasm. As a result, it all got put on the back shelf as I spent the better part of the last 30 years engaged in very left-brained pursuits.

For someone who gets to now reap the benefits of having re-kindled the fire on the right side of my brain later in my adult life, "Moondancing" by Bernadette Smith became an unexpected delight! It's not just a read, it's an activity that awakens my childhood artist and prompts me to engage with her on a more powerful level.

Each awareness, intention, action, and result helps me know myself more through a playful dance with the music of the universe, rather than a tedious method that sends me struggling upstream against it. Most of all, I love that it puts me directly in the driver seat of my own desires AND awakens my creative muse! It contained nuggets of techniques and tips I could directly apply to my creative work as well. Inspiration and instruction all rolled up into a beautiful package that is fun, airy, and light! A must have—in my opinion."

– **Juliette Mansour**, Photographer and Blogger at The Additional f-Stop

"This latest book of Bernadette's shares her uniquely playful formula for harvesting the natural energy of our moon cycles to gently invoke awareness and then action, to create the positive changes we seek in our lives. What a graceful way to move through the components of creating lasting change!"

– **Debra Gamble**, Life Coach

"I feel fortunate to have been part of the 2007 moon cycle manifestation series! What a fulfilling experience. Understanding and utilizing the energies of the different phases of the moon to help me tap more clearly and effectively into the Law of Attraction, into what I really wanted—an opportunity to really know myself—felt like the tool that was missing. It helped me focus and stay present to the moment, to the ebbs and flows of my own energies and those of our world. To sit in awareness, to set intentions, to act on those intentions— all supported by the energy of the moon phases—and then watch the results unfold. When I felt uninspired or stuck, I felt supported in knowing that the group was also doing the same thing … And knowing that the moon in all her glory would continue cycling, and nothing I did or didn't do would stop her, helped me affirm my humanness and know that I could jump back into the cycles at any point if I got sidetracked and once again be supported in manifesting my desires. I love the dance metaphor—so many varieties of steps and twirls to add to the music. Thank you, Bernadette, for your gift to us all!"

– **Laurie R. Oliver**, LMT, Licensed Massage Therapist and
Owner of Life Dance Wellness Center

moondancing

moon dancing

using the cycles of the moon to supercharge
your creativity and manifest your dreams

bernadette rose smith

published by
ENLIGHTENED INK
Covington, Georgia

Cover art and interior design by Bernadette Rose Smith

Originally published as *Moon Cycle Manifesting* for subscriber-only series. ©2007
Excerpts from *Bernadette's Pages: An Intimate Crossroad* ©2006

For information on appearance, workshop or lecture availability,
please contact Bernadette through Enlightened Ink at enlightenedink.com.

Library of Congress Control Number: 2015914080

ISBN: 978-0-9777990-0-8

First Edition: October 2015

"By means of all created things, without exception, the divine assails us, penetrates us, and molds us. We imagined it as distant and inaccessible, when in fact we live steeped in its burning layers."
– Pierre Teilhard de Chardin –

——— • • • ———

This book is dedicated to
all who keep dancing, on the bright side and in the shadows.
Know this; your dance makes a difference.

——— • • • ———

CONTENTS •••

CONTENTS •••

PART TWO: It's Not Just A Phase. Practice. Play It Again.

"And above all, watch with glittering eyes the whole world around you because the greatest secrets are always hidden in the most unlikely places. Those who don't believe in magic will never find it."
– Roald Dahl –

ABOUT THE *dance* ...

Welcome, dear moondancer. I am so happy that you are here.

You arrived just in time to frolic with me under the moonlight and embark on a rhythmic journey toward manifesting your desires by using the cycles of the moon.

The moondancing material you are holding in your hands was originally created for an online subscriber-only series I developed in 2007, after I published my first book, *Bernadette's Pages: An Intimate Crossroad*. For twelve months we danced under the moon all over the world. When the year came to a close, numerous participants asked that I convert this series into a book. So many creative projects and life transitions were set in motion, as a result of the synergy of that time and special group of moondancers, that it has taken me this long to see my way through the moon dust we kicked up!

Having seen the flashing green glow of go—the moon is ever so patient a dance partner—I am ready to sprinkle moonbeams and crank up the music once again. So grab your favorite dancing shoes and allow me the honor of sharing this dance with you.

Love,
Bernadette

supercharge your dreams supercharge your creativity manifest your dreams

"The world is full of magic things,
patiently waiting for our senses to grow sharper."
– W. B. Yeats –

HOW TO *dance* • • •

I want you dancing on the bright side of the moon—not tripping in the dark—so this section gives you the background music you will need to better understand the choreography of the dance. It is my intention to set the stage for you to have an experience that empowers you, not educate you with moon facts or metaphysical meanderings nor inundate you with musts and rules. I am sharing this as a muse would. So you can relax. This moondance is a playful way to tap into and manifest your dreams using the organic progression of moon cycles, creative prompts, and a very simple formula.

a side note for CREATIVE FOLK • • •

If you are drawn to this material hoping to heighten or harvest your creativity, you will find that moondancing prompts easily adapt to personal as well as group creativity challenges. I speak as a creative when I say it is no secret that, as multi-faceted and talented folk, we spend ample time on the moon in our imaginal realm but are challenged with manifesting our talents back on the earth plane. Whether for profit or pleasure, we often lose our rhythm and our joy when it comes to balancing mundane matters with activities that nurture us as artists and writers and musicians … OH MY! (Sorry, I couldn't resist putting on my Wizard of Oz hat there.)

I encourage you to use the moon in a visceral way so your creative impulses have a chance to take root here, where all of us can enjoy what it feels like when you are sharing your gifts and steppin' to the music! Take the seeds from the prompts to create a moondancing piece of art, song, poetry, story, video, collage, or vision board that anchors in your passion and nurtures your creative process as you continue dancing between the heavens and the earth.

your FIRST STEPS •••

As you leaf through the pages of this book you will see that I have set it up to act as a gathering place for your thoughts and discoveries. Yes. I want you to write in it. Color in it. Paste pictures in it. Even cut it up. You will find plenty of blank pages and visual prompts to encourage you. And if this book is not big enough to capture all the moonbeams you will be gathering, cut these pages out, hole punch them, and create a moondancing binder with pockets and tabs and anything else your moondancing feet fancy. If you are an artist, dedicate a visual journal to the dance in addition to this book. Then keep it all handy. You never know when you will be inspired with a little extra time to contemplate some of the ideas we will be exploring. Remember...

what we CoNTeMPLaTe we aCTiVaTe!

the MOON CYCLES •••

Moon cycles provide a rhythm, a visual aid, and a wonderful energy to exponentially charge and keep you moving through the manifestation formula you'll be playing with. Make sure you have a calendar that shows the moon cycles. You will want to pencil in the dates on the line provided beneath each new cycle. This will keep you in step with when to do your prompts.

Prompts will be short, easy activities designed to gently inspire you to creative expression and manifestation. Most will take no more than 15 minutes. You can do them all at once or space them out through the cycle. You can even do just one. The idea is to apply them lightly—not perfectly. Follow your intuition and trust that your subconscious mind will make the connections necessary for you to glean what it is you most need from each prompt and moon cycle. If you have to skip a cycle because "life got messy," don't worry. You can return to this material at any time and will intuitively know where to step back in.

You will be working with three moon cycles—waxing, full, and waning.

Cycle 1. The Waxing Moon: Each waxing moon introduces you to the piece of the manifestation formula you will focus on for all three cycles.

Why use waxing to introduce each piece of the formula? As the moon gets bright, think of an empty glass becoming full. Waxing energy is one of new beginnings. New ideas. It supports absorption and regeneration. This phase of the moon gathers strength, stores energy, makes plans, and so on. Everything you do to fortify yourself is considerably more effective during the waxing moon. Thus, focus on a new idea at this time allows you to absorb more easily the information you are taking in. The energy of the moon supports you. (Did you know that we absorb vitamins and minerals more easily at this time?) The closer you get to the full moon the more powerful this effect becomes which is why...

Cycle 2. The Full Moon: A few days prior to the full moon you will want to reinforce the formula—just in case you forgot or got too busy to focus. The full moon message will give you an extra energy installment toward manifesting your desired goal by tapping into the most powerful absorption energy of the month. By the way, this is a good time to watch what you eat because the body absorbs everything so well—including the many artificial additives put in our food. (This is our highest water retention period so watch the salt moondancers—and all those full moon time-of-the-month cravings, gals!)

Cycle 3. The Waning Moon: The waning moon focuses on releasing that which stands in your way or no longer serves you. The energy of this phase of the darkening moon is one of detoxification, sweating out, expending energy, and springing to action. The further away from the full moon, the more powerful this effect is. The glass that was full now empties. (A good time to clear out that closet!)

the FOUR-PART FORMULA •••
What? You thought I'd give you the formula here without the music? Well, that wouldn't be much fun. (Besides, you probably already peeked.)

This is a formula I use when facilitating Feng Shui Workshops and consulting with clients. It is powerful. It is simple. And it works well in cycles. Each waxing, full, and waning moon cycle will take you deeper into its process of activating the law of attraction through the use of introspective prompts and playful creative expression.

You will be working with one part of the formula through three moon cycles each month. This gives you four months of very doable prompts as your manifestation muscle grows. What this means to you is that you do not have to stop living to follow the moon. Your life can ebb and flow with the cycles (always a good thing) as you play with the formula.

When you have gone through the formula once, I give you the option to cycle back through the formula one more time with fresh thoughts and prompts. (Yes, that is four more months.) Why do this? Because you may want to fine-tune or adjust some of your manifestations—or add a few more dreams to the dance as your understanding deepens.

This four-and-four month schedule is offered as a guideline. I know some of you may want to crank up the music and crash-course this dance into a shorter period of time. In that case, doing all four parts of the formula, in each of the three cycles, will get you to the finish line in one month. Doing two parts of the formula, in each of the three cycles, will get you to the finish line in two months. As your moondance muse I will suggest, however, that you be mindful that you are able to do this in a way that feels balanced or you may find yourself moving so fast that you accidently trip yourself up—as well as what you wish to manifest.

a LITTLE BIT about FENG SHUI •••

Relax. You will not need to run out and get a book on Feng Shui (pronounced Fung Shway) to apply what I share in this moondance. As a matter of fact, when the journal that inspired my first book was written I had never heard of Feng Shui. And yet, I intuitively activated and benefited from its principles during one of the most challenging times of my life. I walked it before I could talk it. And so can you.

As a MuseFusions coach today, I remind folks that energy is responsive. Action taken in one sphere of experience will have an influence on what happens in

another. Think of Feng Shui as the busy work that aligns your signal to that of the genie in the bottle that awaits your request. Thus, some of the moondancing prompts include activities that align with Feng Shui's principles of manifestation.

For those of you who don't know, Feng Shui is often referred to as the Chinese art of placement and has been practiced for thousands of years. Feng Shui, translating as wind-water in English, addresses the dance between the unseen world (wind) and the seen world (water). Its practice applies mindfulness to our relationship with our inner world and witnesses how that reflects in the outer—predominately through our environments and our experiences within them. This is why it makes such a nice dance partner for the moon!

a note about MANIFESTING and GROUP SYNERGY •••

Like the moon, you are creating an energy field that can assist anyone working this formula. Whether you know them or not, others are moondancing with you. Tap into the synergy created by the moondancers' highest intentions as you read each section. It does not matter that you've not been formally introduced as energy resonates within the quantum field of potentiality where we are all connected and none of us are strangers.

Pssst: You might like to form your own moondancing group, and invite friends and family to join you. It is fun to share, support, and harvest together.

is that MuSiC i hear? well, TuRN the PaGe!

———— • • • ————

While her dance on earth bid her stay,
she came to love her feet of clay.
Though they crumbled and caved
in life's tidal wave
of unknowing,
she learned to reshape them
and fire them
with the glowing
golden embers within her heart,
the place that remembered where she got her start
on wings of angels delivered to birth,
royalty not subject
to the mirth
of fault-finders with cast iron feet bound to the earth,
impenetrable and too deep
to leap for the stars,
and catch fireflies in jars
on hot summer nights
when naked feet
find delight
in the dance that bid her stay
while she came to love her feet of clay.

– Bernadette Rose Smith –

Part ONE

FiRST **STePS.**
STaRT THe **MuSiC.**

Here's where we coordinate the formula (*steps*)
with the cycles (*music*) to get those feet tapping happy.

delight in the dance that is your

AWARENESS: *waxing•••*

"My life has a superb cast but I can't figure out the plot."
– Ashleigh Brilliant –

Could manifesting your dreams be as SIMPLE as becoming more aware? Yes. As a matter of fact, it is the key ingredient that super-activates and facilitates the rest of the formula.

Note I said simple, NOT EASY.

Why is that? Well, society does not give us much time to BE in awareness. Consequently, we often find ourselves caught up in reactions—not responses.

What's the difference you ask?

When you react, something outside of you is the cause of your experience. When you respond, something outside of you occurs but you consider yourself part of the equation; thus something within YOU becomes the cause of your experience. You make a choice based on what you know and feel about yourself. This is the difference between victim energy and co-creation.

How does awareness apply to manifesting?

Do I hear the beginning rumblings of grumblings? I know. Awareness seems a bit passive and boring—akin to studying soil content before planting seeds. Who has that kind of time these days, right? Why not go straight to seeding and watering and just see what the harvest brings?

9

Well, you have to know yourself to know if you are really going to like what you think it is that you want—unless you enjoy pulling weeds. Awareness is an assessment tool. A way to inventory what stays and what goes. For example, how much of what you are hoping for or holding onto reflects a past self no longer in existence? (That can be staying in a job you hate as easily as hanging onto a dress you have yet to wear because you bought it a size too small.)

If you don't exercise your option to be aware you are pretty much sitting at the slot machine of potentiality. Maybe you will hit the jackpot. But most times you won't. Do you really want to expend all that time and energy on the "Gee, I hope I like it when I get it" wheel of fortune?

So, where do you start? By becoming aware of how often you ARE and ARE NOT aware. Are you going through your days on autopilot? Days don't seem like much but add them up and they equal your life. Is it one you want?

WAXING **moon** *dance* STEPS•••

Think of this as the new love or romance phase—when everything is fresh and oh so enticing. Fall in love with the MOMENT and just NOTICE what you notice. Don't rush.

Here are a few suggestions to get that awareness muscle flexing for the waxing moon.

• • • Go out tonight and embrace the waxing moon, even if you can't see it. (You can do this during one of those long commercial breaks.) Breathe in the night air. Listen to the night sounds. Feel the moon glow caress your face. Let the moment activate all your senses. Then blow a kiss to the moon and welcome the awareness you'll be gaining before this moon is full. Write down everything your senses pick up and any memory that surfaces with this waxing moon. Don't worry about complete sentences. Just use tag words or phrases. Think of these thoughts as shooting stars dancing around the moon.

● ● ● Pull something out of your closet or drawer that you haven't worn in a while. If you like it, wear it and notice how you feel. If you don't like it, toss it and notice how that makes you feel. Write down everything your senses pick up and any memory this garment triggers. (Like how it got into your closet?) Think of these thoughts as dancing shoes.

● ● ● Next time you're shopping, check the sales clerk's nametag—then look at their eyes. Don't be surprised if they're not looking back. If you hesitate a moment they might look up and make eye contact. If they do, smile and greet them by name. You just encouraged awareness in them as well as yourself. (If they don't engage at all, say a prayer for them. They need one and you'll only benefit.) Write down everything your senses picked up about them and any memories triggered by your exchange. Think of these thoughts as dancing partners.

● ● ● Do not, I repeat, DO NOT LIST any desires, dreams, or wishes yet. Just notice what you notice. Don't rush this process. Remember, awareness counts for the major percentage of the formula.

When we do not take the time to be aware we will find ourselves wanting.

see you near the FuLL mOOn!

aWaReNeSS*musingsdoo*DLeS*photos*FuN

mOREmusingsdooDLeSphotosFuN

mORemusingsdooDLeSphotosFuN

AWARENESS: *full* •••

This cycle's full moon starts on _____

> *"Attention is the rarest and purest form of generosity."*
> – Simone Weil –

Take a breath and feel that full moon rising within your awareness. You are heading into maximum absorption mode.

I share the journal entry below to emphasize how important the awareness part of the formula is, not only on life's fast track but also in times of turmoil and heartache. These are the times when many of us check out and all too often forget to check back in. We numb out. Unplug from a pain that could be intrinsically tied to a creative force—a wake-up call to the abundant flow of life and creation.

This passage marks a decision I made that heralded a time of poignant awareness. My husband was leaving me—for good it seemed. The temptation to play the victim—to remain alert for those who would bless me with their pity, their watery eyes, and their loss of words—was tossed aside with this reflection.

> *"Yesterday, I walked barefoot through the leaves and ate chicken soup sitting on the broken rock wall down by the old fountain. This morning I sat cross-legged on the rug in Lea's bathroom, in front of her full-length mirror. All my make-up spilled out on the floor, like a toy box dumped over. Feeling like a little girl at play. A pixie with a new short haircut, looking back at me in the mirror, painting over her "look what you've done to me" face. On my way home, tonight, I will treat myself to a potted hyacinth—to place by my side of the bed. And in the morning I*

will pick daffodils from our backyard, for a bouquet that will remind me of sunshine yellow days to come.

God, help me to be in the moment and grasp that which has beauty and gives pleasure. Help me to be grateful for the goodness still present in my life."

— *Bernadette's Pages: An Intimate Crossroad*

Reading this today, I still feel the crunching leaves between my toes and the cool rock wall against my thighs. I taste the saltiness of the soup and feel the steamy warmth of the mug in my hands. And yes, I did buy that hyacinth. And I did pick those daffodils. They became powerful symbols reminding me of my decision to be aware—to not compartmentalize my pain, my passion, my creativity—and, as I reflect back, I am deeply grateful for my capacity to choose—a capacity that we all share.

FULL **moon** *dance* STEPS•••

Here are a few more ideas to keep strengthening your awareness muscle as we move into and through the full moon.

●●● Right NOW, look around. What do you SEE? Take it all in. Does it please or displease you? Why? Write down what your senses pick up. Color. Sound. Smell. Taste. Touch. Any memory or story this moment triggers. Don't worry about complete sentences. Just tag words or phrases. And don't censor any repeats from your earlier waxing moon prompts.

●●● Go into your bedroom. What is the first object you notice? How did it find its way into the room? How do you feel about it? (I pray it is not a vacuum cleaner or an ironing board. If it is, we need to talk!) Write down your thoughts and any memory or story that pops up. Or just stay with tag words and phrases.

● ● ●   Pick up a fresh lime. Quarter it and take a big juicy bite. (This will get you in the moment!) Let your senses come alive. How many can you tap into?

● ● ●   Review your earlier writings—waxing through full. Play detective. See any patterns? Any particular focus or emotion? Is there one sense stronger than another? List all these things that awareness is inviting in for you to view. Don't judge whether they are good or bad. Trivial or important. Just let them be what they are and put them on the list.

Now, review the list you just made. Write down any thoughts, memories or stories that rise to the surface. It might be fun to imagine that this is a list made by a new love in your life. What would it tell you about them?

see you near the WaNiNG mOOn!

---

aWaReNeSS *musings* dooDLeS *photos* FuN

_____

_____

_____

_____

_____

_____

_____

_____

_____

_____

aWaReNeSS*musingsdooDLeSphotos*FuN

mORemusingsdooDLeSphotosFuN

mORemusingsdooDLeSphotosFuN

AWARENESS: *waning...*

"Freedom is what you do with what's been done to you."
– Jean-Paul Sartre –

You are now in the release (detox) phase of the moon. I know what you are thinking. That I am going to ask you to list all the things you are now aware of that you do not want. Not quite. Remember you are in the awareness part of the formula, not intention. (Did I say intention? OOPS! That's the next cycle.)

What you are looking for now is awareness of all that stands between you and your *having* awareness! What you want to release with this waning moon—to flush out of your psyche and your lifestyle—are the things that stand between you and awareness.

Maybe it is an attitude that doesn't serve you. Or a fear. An expectation or some sort of performance anxiety. Maybe it's a toxic belief or agenda. Maybe it's the noise from the street or the screaming yellow in your bathroom. Maybe it's a tight waistline. Chronic fatigue. Back pain. An unrealistic schedule...

WANING **moon***dance* STEPS•••

•• • Identify and write down seven things that you would like to release that stand in the way of your being more aware.

•• • Look over that list and pick the top three that do not serve you and highlight them. Write these three on a piece of paper and tape it to your bathroom mirror. As you feel (and see) the moon wane, contemplate your top three picks.

•• • When you look in the mirror each morning, state calmly and with assurance, *"I am open to release."* Breathe in the releasing energy the moon offers and on your exhale affirm, *"I am open to release* _____*"* for each of your three picks.

in the next cycle, the WaXiNG mOOn invites us to focus on the power of iNTeNTioN!

"WHaTNoTs ZoNe"
for sketches, photos, treasure envelope, or whatever you like!

aWaReNeSS*musingsdooDLeSphotos*FuN

mORe*musings*dooDLeS*photos*FuN

INTENTION: *waxing* •••

"Find out who you are and do it on purpose."
– Dolly Parton –

in•ten•tion The Webster's New World Dictionary defines intention as *"A determination to act in a specified way."* (Hmmm. Short and to the point but not very exciting.) Determination. Let's look that one up. *"Firmness of purpose."* Sounds like work. And indeed it is without awareness.

Without awareness we find ourselves abundantly well intentioned. (Isn't there a road to hell somewhere, paved with good intentions?) So, why is that? Applying intention without awareness is like using a road map with no destination in mind. We find ourselves traveling to a lot of places that we may not want to visit—unless it was our intention to meander. (Sorry, I couldn't resist.) If intention enlists so much power when it meets with the law of attraction wouldn't we like to know where we are going? Or at least know how we got there if it's not to our liking?

I have a little game I play whenever I find myself considering a major change; like a move for example. I ask, *"Based on what I know about myself as I am now and how I would like to see myself a year from now, what kind of environment ... house, community, friendships, lifestyle ... would support me moving in that direction?"* I make out a list and determine (there's that word) what would best support my meeting that goal–that vision of self. Then I play. I pretend. I shop the universe.

A deceptively simple but critical question. Dissect it.

Based on what I know about myself as I am now (awareness) and how I would like to see myself a year from now (intention), what kind of environment ... house, community, friendships, lifestyle ... would support me moving in that direction? (A determination to act in a specified way.)

Now, this creates a list that will take you places. Could I tell you some amazing stories? You bet!

WAXING **moon** *dance* STEPS•••

What are you going to do during this waxing moon, this time of readily absorbing new ideas and approaches? You are going to flex your awareness and intention muscles and ask yourself the same question.

••• List seven things that you know about yourself as you are today. (Love gardening. Hate snow. Easily distracted. Caregiver. Voracious reader. Frustrated musician...)

••• Then list—determine—how you would like to see yourself a year from now.

••• Now, play with blending your two lists. Pretend. Mentally shop for the environment that will support you moving in that direction. And remember, environment can refer to your inner terrain—emotional and spiritual—as well.

> *For example:* If you love to draw and haven't in a long while, what would it take to get you moving? Joining a local artist's guild so you can exchange information and inspiration? Put that on your list. Ordering pizza and inviting friends over to help you clear out that junk room so you can set up a studio? Write that down, too. Get the picture?

Go about this lightly. This is not about coming up with the perfect list and setting out to execute it perfectly. Just PLAY with it!

see you near the FuLL mOOn!

iNTeNTioN*musings*dooDLeS*photos*FuN

iNTeNTioNmusingsdooDLeSphotosFuN

mOREmusingsdooDLeSphotosFuN

mOR*emusings*dooDLe*Sphotos*FuN

INTENTION: *full* ...

This cycle's full moon starts on _____

> *"Don't be satisfied with stories, how things have gone with others.*
> *Unfold your own myth."*
> *– Rumi –*

Feel that full moon? We are heading into the maximum absorption phase.

> *"You have always looked to [others] to place your value. You must value you.*
> *How else will you know what, in your experience, is worth the attention and so*
> *the intention that you give? It is intentions that create your life experience.*
> *Where would misdirected or misunderstood intentions place your life?"*
>
> *– Spirit Dialog, Bernadette's Pages: An Intimate Crossroad*

Go back to Webster's definition for intention. *"A determination to act in a specified way."* What does it mean to move with determination? (Determination is such a determined word.) You actually have to determine a direction to go in. Is this a direction that is self-perpetuating, based on what you know about yourself? Are you part of the equation? Or are you bouncing, like a ping-pong ball, off something that occurs outside you? Or worse yet, like a ricocheting bullet?

Why does it matter? Spirit stated it in the excerpt above.

> *"It is intentions that create your life experience. Where would misdirected or*
> *misunderstood intentions place your life?"*

I know where they placed mine at that time and Spirit was right. I didn't like it a bit. Where I had been focusing my attention became my *intention-by-default*, creating a constant interference pattern between where I was and where I wanted to be.

Determination + specificity = intention. Determination born of specificity creates an intention that leads to an action. So, intention has to be fueled by more than a want or a wish. It is a determination.

"...WHAT, in your experience, is worth the attention and so the intention that you give?"

Now do you see why you also need to flex that awareness muscle? Because if you really want to successfully create a reality that suits you, you have to know a few things beyond "I want."

FULL **moon**dance STEPS•••

••• As you observe the moon reaching its fullest potential, review your lists from the waxing moon and see if you feel called to refine or add to them.

••• Check for any misdirected or misunderstood "blending" of intentions and re-adjust their course.

••• Pick one thing, one intention that you would like to focus on. Highlight it. Give it your full attention as you enlist the receptive energy of the full moon. (Don't worry. You'll get to the others.)

see you near the WaNiNG mOOn!

iNTeNTioN*musings*dooDLeS*photos*FuN

mORemusingsdooDLeSphotosFuN

INTENTION: *waning*•••

"Life is full and overflowing with the new.
But it is necessary to empty out the old to make room for the new to enter."
– Eileen Caddy –

Here we are at the releasing phase of the moon. What shall you purge with this one? How about misdirected intentions? But how do you determine them? I have a clue for you, an easy way to uncover misdirected intentions. What are you worrying about? (Obsessing on, if you will.) What has captured your attention?

Remember: *"WHAT, in your experience, is worth the attention and so the intention that you give?"*

Let's release those ***intentions-by-default***, those obsessions of the mind that fuel your journey through disappointment, frustration, and loss. Or, to look at it another way—those in a recovery program should know this one—that which you think about most becomes your Higher Power. And guess what? That is the universe where you get to live and move and have your being. Nuff said?

WANING **moon***dance* STEPS•••

This is what you are going to do during the waning moon.

●●● Go to the one intention from your list that you decided to give your full attention to. Interrogate it. Did it come from within or without? Is it a reaction or a response? Did it find its birth in a worry?

> *For example:* You are in debt. You decide to go back to school so you can make more money. (Good) But you select a field you are ambivalent about, expecting its six-figure income to cure your worries. (Do you see an intention-by-default here?) You are focusing on lack—something outside of you. With lack as your fuel, chances are good that six-figures will find their way to you in the form of school loans + interest + living expenses with no position available when you graduate. (Law of attraction. You got your six-figures as seen through the lens of lack. The one you were looking through when you set your intention.)

●●● Don't throw out the baby with the bath water just yet. Can you re-frame your intention? What do I mean? Look at it through another lens. I once knew a woman who went to school in her late thirties to become a lawyer. After investing a lot of money—and a lot of energy, balancing school with two kids and a husband—she decided law was not for her. Not for any kind of money. She had a brilliant mind and would have been a great lawyer, but decided to help people by becoming a counselor instead. Her brilliant mind followed her heart. No doubt many are grateful she made that choice.

This moon phase supports purging and releasing. Purify your intention as mindfully as you can before you take action. Did I say action? Yes!

**next cycle's piece of the formula is aCTioN,
where you get to throw a little Feng Shui into the pot!**

iNTeNTioN *musings* dooDLeS *photos* FuN

mOREmusingsdooDLeSphotosFuN

ACTION: *waxing* •••

This cycle's waxing moon starts on _____

"The man who moves a mountain begins by carrying away small stones."
– Chinese Proverb –

Action. It's about time, eh? This is the part of the formula where we typically divide into two groups. Group one will ask why action is the final part of the formula and not the first: Can't we just fine-tune as we go? Group two will ask why we have to spoil a perfectly good formula with action: Can't we just think ourselves into manifesting what we want?

That depends. How much time and energy do you want to spend? Awareness, intention, and action—combined mindfully—bring out the best in each other and make for a very efficient team. I appreciate efficiency when it comes to manifesting happiness in my life. I love those miraculous, serendipitous moments that lift my spirit and make smooth my path. And I am guessing you do, too.

Here we are well into the waxing moon—the moon of new views and new beginnings. So, what action is called for? Look at your list of intentions. Are you noticing that a few of the intentions are not new to you? Now look at your list of awareness. Ask yourself where you may have applied intention and action without awareness, or awareness and action without intention, or action with no awareness or intention. Get the picture?

What would it look like to apply the whole formula? Allow that idea to seep into your consciousness as you consider the one intention you selected to focus on last cycle. Ask yourself what action you would apply to that intention now, based on the awareness you have gained.

Perhaps the first action you see is not practical at the moment. (You're not ready to quit your job.) Here is where a little bit of the power of Feng Shui comes in. There are all kinds of actions—Feng Shui adjustments—that you can busy yourself with that will prepare the quantum field for the seed of intention you wish to plant.

WAXING **moon** *dance* STEPS•••

This waxing moon is a great time to activate the wisdom area of your home's bagua. (Pronounced bogwa.) If you are Feng Shui literate you already know where that is. The rest of you, who do not know what I am talking about, select any area within your home that you feel drawn to and claim it as your wisdom area for the duration of this dance step. If you share space with a roommate you might want to choose an area that is predominately yours.

Now you are ready to apply an ancient Feng Shui cure—to mindfully adjust your designated place of wisdom with awareness, intention, and action. One simple action to activate the quantum field of possibilities on your behalf is all that is required of you at this time.

••• Buy a helium balloon that says "Congratulations"—Congrats, Well Done, or Good Job will also serve our purpose—and place it within your designated wisdom area. Yes, you read that right. (Don't balk now. You've come this far.)

Okay, maybe a helium balloon is not exactly ancient but this mindful application is. Come on. Think about it just a little. Maybe the sales clerk asks you whom the balloon is for. Imagine the curious smile they might have on their face when you say "me." Or, imagine you are walking out of the store with your balloon bobbing over your head. Everyone who sees it can't help offering energy in response to the subliminal message of congratulations that it sends. Feel that energy grow?

Your balloon affirms you, your success, and every person who witnesses its cheery message. How powerful is that? And you will have to smile, or at least chuckle a little, every time you see it bobbing around within your wisdom area. (If for no other reason than you can't believe you actually bought into the idea of using a balloon as a Feng Shui cure.) Understand that every time you smile, you are opening more channels for the law of attraction to do its thing. On a subconscious level you are seeing and feeling your desire as already accomplished. Get the picture? (Advertisers use subliminal messages all the time because they work.)

● ● ● *Now, go out and buy that balloon!* A little action goes a long way when done mindfully with awareness and intention. You are activating your energy field of wisdom with an image of celebration and success. Pay attention. Notice how you feel. Capture your observations in this journal and definitely note any insights, guidance, synchronicities, or opportunities for clarification that support your intention.

see you near the FuLL mOOn!

"WHaTNoTs ZoNe"
for quotes, fortune cookie messages, lottery tickets, or whatever you like!

aCTioN*musings*dooDLeS*photos*FuN

ACTION: *full* •••

"Do not let your fire go out, spark by irreplaceable spark in the hopeless swaps of the not-quite, the not-yet, and the not-at-all. Do not let the hero in your soul perish in lonely frustration for the life you deserved and have never been able to reach. The world you desire can be won. It exists ... it is real ... it is possible ... it's yours."

– Ayn Rand –

Feel that full moon rising within your awareness as you head into maximum absorption mode. By now your balloon has done its job and is ready to be relieved of its duty.

"I find myself cleaning up the entrance to my little bungalow. Planting impatiens on either side of the old brick steps, spreading fresh bales of pine straw, pruning the bushes along the walkway, and obsessing on finding the perfect purple to paint my screen door. As if to say, "Hey world, look at me emerging from the ashes!" The poor guy at the paint store could probably have done with seeing less of me. Polite exasperation with a tinge of curiosity was his hue when I showed up for the third time with quart in hand. According to him, the base could not take any more pigment and I was going to have to start over from scratch or settle. I am pretty sure I detected a sigh of relief when I decided to go with what I had. It still doesn't match the purple I see in my head, but my door is a big hit with Angie's kids.

I feel the shift has occurred and is making its way to consciousness and the physical realm. Thus the quest for my perfectly expressive door!"

– Bernadette's Pages: An Intimate Crossroad

When it comes to the law of attraction, is there really any difference between purple doors and helium balloons? (No doubt, my neighbors at that time would have thought so!) Written just three months after the break up of my eighteen-year marriage, this passage illustrates how amazing things can happen when action follows awareness and intention. What is so amazing about a purple screen door? Look at the passage again. There is humor and hope between the lines. Anyone who has been left for another knows how amazing that is.

Awareness. Intention. Action. Three months of one intense awareness after another, of replacing intentions-by-default with intentions based on self-discovery. Three months that led to the sudden inspiration to paint my screen door purple. What did that purple door say to me? What were its subliminal messages? Well, there was no arguing with its greeting as I pulled in the driveway from work. Unique in a neighborhood of green, white, and black doors, it did not suffer with my invisibility issues. It did not apologize or accept shame for a failed marriage. All that with a purple door? You bet. And next month, when I tell you what part of the bagua that door was in and what I attracted into my life—all without knowing Feng Shui—you will be convinced that Feng Shui adjustments are a great way to stimulate the law of attraction. *You are already doing it.*

FULL **moon** *dance* STEPS•••

So, during this full moon, what action shall you take on behalf of the intention you decided to focus on? *Hmmm.* Three ideas come to mind, each addressing a different phase of readiness. Pick one that suits where you are. (Or do them all.)

• • • This one is fun and very powerful by itself or as a support for suggestions two and three: You will need a blank note card or greeting card and envelope—preferably something not too small. A couple of magazines—you may want magazines specific to your intention—scissors, glue, and a stamp.

Are you ready? Clip pictures and words out of your magazines that support your specific intention as if it has *already* happened—enough to cover the front, inside, and back with a collage of these clippings. As you are pasting them on, imagine you are on a trip and sending these photos and captions to someone you love to show them where you are and to convince them that they need to hop on the next plane to join you!

When you finish, address the envelope to yourself. The return address will be your current address but identify yourself as the sender with a title that supports your intention. (Dr. Josephine Esteem, Sculpture Extraordinaire Bill...) See, this is coming from your future self who has already arrived. Get the picture? Stamp it and drop it in the mail. ***You have to mail it!*** This activity can move you into an altered state so I suggest doing this when you know you are not going to be driving immediately afterward.

● ● ● Here's a Feng Shui Adjustment: Place one of these symbolic objects, with intention and awareness, in an appropriate place within the pre-designated wisdom area of your home: A candle (illumination), a plant (growth), a book (representing wisdom), a photo (of someone whose wisdom you aspire to), or a vase of flowers (harvest). If there is no available space in which to affirm your wisdom with one of these objects you may have a clutter challenge that needs to go on your awareness-intention-action list!

● ● ● A specific action toward your goal: Having trouble seeing yourself taking the action? Think out of the box! Want to get into the medical field and work in a hospital? Visit a local hospital. Pray in the chapel. Volunteer in the gift shop. Eat in the cafeteria. (You may as well get used to the food now.) Want to go back to school to further your education? Contact a school and ask for their information packet. Something you can hold in your hands and place in your wisdom area. Hang out at a local campus library. Attend a local university function. Research for a grant. Get the idea?

see you near the WaNiNG mOOn!

aCTioNmusingsdooDLeSphotosFuN

ACTION: *waning* •••

This cycle's waning moon starts on _____

"Light happens. Be ready. Ride the light and find inspiration in your shadows."
– ME –

Here we are at the releasing phase of the moon. It is time to select an action that significantly represents purging whatever is standing between you and harvesting positive results from your chosen intention.

In the twelve-step recovery program of AA there are two action steps that pave the way for alcoholics to release what stands between them and the life they wish to maintain. Step 8 says: *"Made a list of all persons we had harmed, and became willing to make amends to them all."* (Many recovering alcoholics are told to include themselves on this list.) Step 9 says: *"Made direct amends to such people wherever possible, except when to do so would injure them or others."*

The dictionary identifies the word "amend" as a verb, an action word—to correct, improve, change or revise. Add "s" and amend turns into amends, a noun—action manifests into form. In this case, the form of a payment made or satisfaction given for injury or loss.

If you are not in a recovery program, you are probably wondering where I am going with this. Well, there is a profound wisdom expressed in these two steps. The principles behind this process of making amends not only leads you to a greater happiness and freedom but also helps you maintain a lifestyle that is not a compromised version of your past.

It has been my observation that when someone has difficulty achieving a result they want quite often there is some guilt—thus fear—cruising the neighborhood. To amend (correct) the situation there is a need to backtrack, find the guilt and the fear it supports, and re-direct through forgiveness—then move forward.

I know, this part of the action phase does not sound like it is going to be as much fun as helium balloons and collage note cards but make no mistake, this is where the rubber hits the road when it comes to getting results.

WANING **moon** *dance* STEPS•••

Now, here are a few more suggested action steps for the waning moon. Focusing on your chosen intention:

●●● Make a list: Any experience or feeling that resonates with your "missing the mark," in respect to your intention, goes on this list. (I have to do this to make up for a bad marriage—loss. I went bankrupt in my last business venture—shame.) Get the picture?

●●● Make another list: Anyone whose life would be affected by the harvesting of your intention. Harvesting can shift relationships in unexpected ways. What do you think their responses will be? Any, *"Who do you think you are"* dialogs come to surface? Or how about, *"You've changed."* Or maybe, *"You don't have time for me anymore."*

●●● As you look at these two lists, ask yourself: Am I willing to forgive the guilt? Am I willing to release the fear? (I am not asking you to forgive or to release. I am asking you to focus on your willingness.) When you come to that feeling of willingness write, *"I am willing,"* with soap or lipstick, on your bathroom mirror. Why the bathroom? Because it is a good place to purge!

Focus on the releasing energy of the moon. Take a deep breath and hold it as long as you comfortably can. On your exhale, affirm, *"I am willing."* Take another deep breath and hold it as long as you can. On your exhale, affirm, *"I am willing to forgive myself."* Take one more deep breath. Hold it. And on your exhale, affirm, *"I am willing to release my fear."*

● ● ● For those of you who want to take more physical action: Purge three objects from your home that reinforce guilt, fear, or failure. Or three objects that reinforce unsupportive relationships. (Sorry! These objects have to be yours. So, don't get any ideas about tossing something tacky that your ex sent home with your daughter.) Here is an example, from my book, of a purging action I took just before my husband moved out.

> *Last night I tore up the copy of The Artist's Way that he gave me. Page by page. I was so methodical. So angry. It was almost scary. I didn't know the woman who could do this. I couldn't control her. Scribbled commentaries, in crayon, on the pages. Things I have been wanting to say to him but haven't. ... I am not letting him have any part of my artist self. I am accepting no contributions from him ... I packed up all our special love trinkets. ... Tossed The Artist's Way pages on top ... He can take it all with him.*

Now, I admit that was a bit dramatic. (I had a lot of guilt and fear that I had not yet dealt with.) And I don't generally recommend tearing up books as an action step— unless it's for an art project—but this excerpt shows how you can get creative with your action.

in the next cycle, the WaXiNG mOOn invites us to focus on ReSuLTS!

aCTioNmusingsdooDLeSphotosFuN

mORemusingsdooDLeSphotosFuN

mORe*musings*dooDLeS*photos*FuN

RESULTS: *waxing*•••

"The road to enlightenment is long and difficult,
and you should try not to forget snacks and magazines."
– Anne Lamott –

What can I possibly say about results? I mean, the formula is done after you apply awareness, intention, and action. Right? Results are results. Or are they?

This is where many of us can get lost. Which is why I want you to think of a result as a point on a map. For example: How much does that point tell you about all there is to experience in Santa Fe, New Mexico? That point encompasses a lot of territory. But what does that point define? If you live in Santa Fe, it defines everything. If you do not, it defines nothing truly usable as a personal experience.

It's important to remember, when you are working a formula like this, results are not the destination. They are a part of the journey. You do not take up permanent residence with a result.

This is the part of the formula where you pay attention, like you would if you were driving into Santa Fe for the first time. Results (the arrival zone) now call for more awareness (watch those street signs), clarified intention (decide what you want to see and do in this new terrain), and fine-tuned action (turn right at the big chicken).

Sometimes you hit your target on the first try with this formula. But many times you do not. Does that mean you failed to work the formula properly? No. Is this a good time to exercise your faith muscle and trust in divine order? Yes. Absolutely.

> *"For everyone that asketh receiveth; and he that seeketh findeth; and to him that knocketh it shall be opened. Or what man is there of you, whom if his son ask bread, will he give him a stone"* – Matthew 7: 8–9

WAXING **moon** *dance* STEPS•••

As the moon gains in fullness, look for synchronicities—occurrences that point the way and affirm your path.

Ever wake with a song verse stuck in your head? Spot a billboard on the highway with a phrase that jumps out at you? (I have received many a message from a billboard or an advertisement on the side of an 18-wheeler.) Perhaps a friend gifts you with a book, or an unexpected opportunity allows you to travel on the job. These little signposts—results—help to fine-tune your focus. They also encourage a playful kind of patience should you discover there are a few extra steps you need to take before you can experience your heart's desire.

••• *Create a Synchronicity Journal:* I encourage you to create a synchronicity journal. Not just for present synchronicities, but also for any time a strange coincidence occurred in response to a situation in which you needed or called for assistance. Past or present—any synchronicity counts for this journal.

This can be a small journal or tablet—easily carried in your purse or pocket—in which you write one synchronicity per page. This format allows you to recapture each moment at a glance and helps to beef up your faith muscle when divine order calls for a little more time and patience than you were planning to expend. It also helps you hone your intuition. Trust me. I know from personal experience how helpful it can be to have a litany of synchronicities to call forth when there seems to be a "hush" in response to an intention!

see you near the FuLL mOOn!

ReSuLTs*musings*dooDLeS*photos*FuN

mORemusingsdooDLeSphotosFuN

RESULTS: *full* ...

> *"Every exit is an entry somewhere else."*
> *– Tom Stoppard –*

You will recall, during the full moon phase of Action, I shared a story from my book about painting my front door purple. Though I knew nothing about Feng Shui at the time, that story acts as a witness to what can happen when awareness, intention, and action are applied.

As a Feng Shui practitioner, I love working with the bagua. (Remember your designated wisdom area earlier?) The bagua maps out nine areas of concern—self, career, wisdom, health, wealth, fame, love, creativity, networking and travel—that contribute to or deplete from your wellness and joy. Think of it as a blueprint for your home. But instead of showing you the location of a bedroom or closet, it reveals the area that "claims" one of these life concerns. In Feng Shui, you adjust areas of the bagua when you wish to encourage support of a specific intention or desire.

What is so amazing about the action I took to paint my door purple? (A color that cultivates intuition and spirituality, by the way.) When I tell you what part of the bagua my door was in and what I attracted into my life, you will see why Feng Shui is a great way to stimulate the law of attraction. The following excerpts illustrate the power of awareness and intention.

This was written in March, three days after my husband moved out.

> *"I have to find a new job. Something fun that will capture and hold my attention.*
> *Break me out of this rut that is so much a reminder of [us] ... I'm afraid my artist's*
> *block will dig in even deeper. I need a comfort base to create from but I'm not sure*
> *what that would look like ... It's time to stop denying myself ... To make my own*
> *discoveries. To create an environment that supports and reflects this woman who*
> *is unfolding."*

This was written in June, not long after painting my door purple.

> *"Would have called in sick today if there had been someone to call in to. It's rough,*
> *managing the showroom on days like this. No one here to sub for me. A boss who*
> *lives out of state. I feel trapped. Isolated. The halls are empty. Not a single buyer*
> *and the morning is almost over.*
>
> *This showroom looks so trashy. Everything I do to improve its appearance, Joel*
> *undoes when he comes through town. It never occurs to him to ask why I display*
> *product the way I do. My background in art and design, my understanding of*
> *color—all invisible to him. I am left to work around his chaotic hit and run*
> *arrangements. Replicas of antique guns and swords displayed with lace, dollhouse*
> *furniture, and Mother's day plaques! Good Lord. I need to find something to do*
> *that I will feel good about and appreciated for ... What is it with these men? Am I*
> *so insignificant? Why do I reflect this back to myself?"*

Something I struggled with long before my husband left—and continued to struggle with some time after—was how to integrate my livelihood with my creativity and passion. To put it another way; at the age of thirty-nine, I didn't know what I wanted to be when I grew up.

Results! I wrote this next entry in mid-July, just two months after painting my door purple. With minimal effort to find another job, I literally stumbled into this opportunity.

> *"So much to write about, but no time! The interview went well. I start my new job*
> *in August. Production coordinator. It's not exactly back in advertising, but I will*

have to use my advertising experience to coordinate layout, design, pre-press, and printing with product deadlines. Going to be wearing a lot of hats ... with a job that will stimulate my mind ..."

Now I will tell you where that purple door was in my bagua—if you have not already guessed it. Career! Though this position did not turn out to be my life's work, it certainly answered to many of my needs at that time—body, mind, and spirit. And it turned out to be my "last stop" before springboarding into what I do today.

FULL **moon***dance* STEPS•••

As you enjoy the full moon, continue to notice, recall, and record synchronicities in your journal. You might even like to decorate some of your pages with doodles, photos or magazine clippings to visually strengthen a particular synchronicity. Have fun with it!

see you near the WaNiNG mOOn!

paste an envelope here to gather SYNCHRoNiCiTY CLiPpiNGs!

ReSuLTs*musings*dooDLeS*photos*FuN

RESULTS: *waning*•••

This cycle's waning moon starts on _____

"It is not what men eat, but what they digest, that makes them strong,
not what we gain, but what we save, that makes us rich,
not what we read, but what we absorb, that makes us learned,
not what we preach, but what we practice, that makes us lovable."
– Francis Bacon –

Results and the releasing phase of the moon. What do you do with this one? Releasing always seems to be the more challenging task. (At least that is what my clutter clients tell me.) And once you have a result, well, there is no purging it. Right?

Not necessarily. Results you don't care for can be transmuted. Recycled. How? By releasing your attachment to outcome. Why? Because your attachment to outcome comes with opinions, and opinions are judgments flying under radar. (Bet you never thought of an opinion that way.) And judgments under radar—or not—have to be supported and defended. Like a high maintenance relationship, they eat up a lot of emotional and physical energy. Energy that could be directed more constructively. (Just my opinion. Ha!)

There was an author I enjoyed back in the 80's. His name was Jess Lair. One of his books was entitled *I Don't Know Where I'm Going, But I Sure Ain't Lost.* In it, he had a line that I always loved—and still use to this day. *"Don't seek truth, just stop having opinions."* Profound in its simplicity but not so easy to do. There are many days when I prefer to delude myself, thinking I can more successfully find the truth than release an opinion.

What does your attachment to outcome and opinions have to do with results and the waning moon?

Think about your intention. How many opinions do you have about what you think your result should look like? Behave like? Feel like? Bet you have a few more opinions—thus attachments—than you thought. Maybe one is; where it should happen. Or how about; when it should happen. Or even; how long you should wait for it to happen before you quit and throw in the towel.

Letting go of our need to view a result through the eyes of an opinion—that destination point we talked about during the waxing moon—allows us to intuitively sense the bigger picture. Allows us to trust our resources. And, as we gain in trust, we experience more opportunities where we feel supported. Loosening our grip on attachment to outcome frees us from opinions and judgments that do not serve us. Now the "less than hoped for" results transmute into learning tools that can be used to make adjustments where necessary as we continue our journey.

What was that you said? How do we work the formula, state an intention, and visualize a result without having an opinion? Don't we need opinions to determine what experiences or possessions we want—or don't want—to have?

When we have no opinions—well, okay, fewer opinions—we lose our attachments, attachments that really witness to an imbalance of mind over spirit. Ask anyone who has struggled with an addiction where their attachments and opinions led them and if they were happy with the results.

What we are looking for here is a healthier way to assess our results, thus determine our desires. Why? Because the result part of any law of attraction formula is actually the trickiest. In my opinion—chuckle snort—this is where most folks get tripped up and become disenchanted, bitter, or quit. All because of the opinions, judgments, and expectations they held to as their assessment lens. This is why it is so important that we cast the light on our "judgments flying under radar." Because when THEY strike, we usually do not know what hit us.

WANING **moon***dance* STEPS...

What opinions can you release during the waning phase of this moon? Look for any opinions that you have. Yes, ANY. They don't have to be attached to your work with this formula.

● ● ● Then ask:

1. Does this opinion serve me?

2. Do I feel better for having or holding this opinion?

If your answer is no to either of these questions, release the opinion. (Note I said either.)

Focus on the releasing energy of the moon. Take a deep breath and hold it as long as you comfortably can. On your exhale, affirm, *"I am willing."* Take another deep breath and hold it as long as you can. On your exhale, affirm, *"I am willing to release this opinion."* Take one more deep breath. Hold it. And on your exhale, affirm, *"I am willing to release this attachment."*

● ● ● For those of you who want a visual reminder: Light a white 7-day candle and, as you watch the candle burn down, imagine that it is burning away any opinions that do not serve you.

next moon cycle we go more deeply into aWaReNeSS.

ReSuLTsmusingsdooDLeSphotosFuN

mORemusingsdooDLeSphotosFuN

results • results • results • results • results

mORe*musings*dooDLeS*photos*FuN

iT's NoT JuST a **pHaSe.** PRaCTiCe. PLaY iT **AGaiN.**

One. Two. Three. One. Two. Three.
Now relax, turn up the volume, and let's dance some more.

"WHaTNoTs ZoNe"
for sketches, photos, treasure envelope, or whatever you like!

AWARENESS: *waxing•••*

This cycle's waxing moon starts on _____

"An artist is not paid for his labor but for his vision."
– James Whistler –

As many of you know, I am an artist. In my world as an artist there is something called a viewfinder. It is a neat little gadget that artists use to practice seeing. A viewfinder frames a scene and, in doing so, increases the artist's awareness of light, shadow, shape, color, and composition. It provides a context within which an artist sees. A lot for an amazingly simple device.

I refer to it as a visioning tool; a tool that takes me from **assuming** a scene to truly being in the essence of a scene. As a result of this kind of SEEING, I am able to energetically capture the moment I choose to express through my art and share my unique—sometimes peculiar—view of the world.

So what, you ask, does this have to do with awareness as it relates to manifestation? Remember...

> *"... you have to know yourself to know if you are even going to like what you think it is that you want. Awareness is an assessment tool. A way to inventory what stays and what goes ... If you don't exercise your option to be aware you are pretty much sitting at the slot machine of potentiality. Maybe you will hit the jackpot. But most times you won't. Do you really want to expend all that time and energy on the "Gee, I hope I like it when I get it" wheel of fortune?"*
>
> *– Part One: Awareness: Waxing*

It is time to flex your awareness muscle. Only this time you will shift from the awareness exercised through simple observation, covered in Part One, to an awareness exercised through contemplative viewing. In the world of the artist, this represents the difference between merely looking at a subject to paint and truly seeing it—a distinction that transforms a doodle into a masterpiece. In manifestation practices, this kind of awareness allows you to fine tune your intention and action. A handy talent to acquire, especially since you don't always manifest the result you are looking for on the first try. I use this kind of awareness as my viewfinder when I work in a client's home. It gives me the "Feng Shui eyes" needed to determine an action that will set an intention.

WAXING **moon***dance* STEPS•••

In this waxing phase of the moon, fresh with new ideas and views, you are going to flex your awareness muscle by engaging your creative eye while playing with your own viewfinder.

Use your viewfinder to increase your awareness between now and the full moon. It also works as a wonderful meditative tool if you find it hard to be still. At least once a day, take 5 minutes to "frame" and "reframe." With just a little bit of practice you will start to feel a shift in your ability to focus. You might even notice some heightened intuition.

●●● You will need to:

Get a sheet of black paper or poster board, a ruler, and a pair of scissors.

Take your black paper or poster board, measure and cut a 6"x 6" square. (A good travel size. Hint. Hint.)

Cut out a 2"x 3" window within the square. (Chill. This doesn't have to be perfect.)

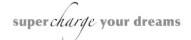

For those of you intimidated by rulers and scissors, go to your local hobby or art store and buy a small viewfinder. Don't miss out on the fun!

Viewfinder in hand, pick an object to frame. Close one eye as you look through the viewfinder. Now take a moment to SEE this object. Move the viewfinder right then left, near then far, and see how your object changes in relationship to what is within the intimate format of the frame. What do you see? How do you feel about what you are seeing?

Don't limit yourself to framing pretty things. Even a pile of dirty laundry develops a mystique with this little device. Try it!

Frame a pet with your viewfinder. A group of children playing. A loved one deep in thought. You will find this does not feel the same as looking at them through a camera lens.

see you near the FuLL mOOn!

paste an eNVeLoPE PoCKeT here for your VieWFiNdeR!

aWaReNeSSmusingsdooDLeSphotosFuN

AWARENESS: *full* •••

"Vision is the art of seeing what is invisible to others."
– Jonathan Swift –

Feel the moon rising within your awareness as it moves into maximum absorption mode, and accept the support this full moon offers for manifesting your desires.

By now you should be fairly proficient with the viewfinder you made. You are going to continue with this theme for the full moon—but with a slight twist. Now, you are going to work with your emotional viewfinder.

Hmmm, you say? How's that?

Remember when I said that a viewfinder offers the artist a context within which to SEE? And how SEEING is the difference between a scribble and a masterpiece? Well, the work you do with your emotional viewfinder determines your ability to frame and re-frame events—thus results—as they occur. This is important in manifestation practices. Especially when you find yourself gathering opinions about the results you are, or are not, getting. An opinion is a perceptual tool that locks you into a specific focus. If you are hoping for a masterpiece—or at least a bit more than a doodle—an opinion that clouds your vision will not serve you well.

Honing awareness while initially choosing an intention and an action to support that intention is often easier before the results come in. But what do you do when your result is not what you expected? Or has not yet appeared?

This is where working with your emotional viewfinder comes in handy.

FULL **moon***dance* STEPS•••

The Emotional Viewfinder: The good news is that you won't have to make this one. You already have it. The question here is how you have been using it.

••• Pull out the viewfinder you made for the last moon phase and focus on the frame only. Close your eyes and hold the image of the frame in your mind. Now think of an event that you have strong feelings about. The birth of a child, a wedding, a divorce, a world event—anything that you have an emotional charge attached to.

Got it? Now frame that event in your mind's eye with your viewfinder. Turn the sound off and let this just be a visual, like a silent movie. Move your frame in then out. Right then left. Onto one character, or group, then another. You can compose the images within the frame or just see what volunteers. It might help to imagine that you are a director of a movie, viewing the day's shoot.

As you continue to use your mental viewfinder, turn up the sound and get involved with your chosen event. How do you feel? Notice any opinions rising to the surface about the feelings you are having? If this is an emotionally challenging event, I invite you to consider viewing it from another angle. Imagine that you can shift your viewfinder to compose a more empowering perspective.

What do I mean? Not so easy you say? Let me share an example of how my viewfinder was shifted *for me* shortly after my husband left to be with another woman. I was in meditation, praying...

> *"... to feel some peace. Closing my eyes, I imagined myself sitting on the grassy bank of a pond nestled deep within a forest and was settling into the tranquility of*

the place when three guides greeted me and told me to visualize scenes from my past, with him, that I would like to heal. So, I went to a few ... Next, I found myself in a misty kind of place with two figures standing maybe ten feet in front of me. It soon became clear that I was looking at [them] in an embrace. As they hugged, I tried to vaporize her out of his arms and out of my meditation, but she just came back and reached for my hand. I was not prepared for the tremendous outpouring of love I felt coming from her, nor the gratitude and love I felt for her.
I was shocked. There was no stopping the exchange of feeling between us. She took my hand and joined it with his. She hugged us both. I saw her gift. I knew it without a doubt. The emotion was overwhelming. I still feel it as I write this.
I know that she is my friend."

– Bernadette's Pages: An Intimate Crossroad

What a powerful shift in perspective that was! And a great "how to" for using an emotional viewfinder in day-to-day events. Granted, that one was given to me but its application is usable to this day with any event, result, or delay that challenges me.

Need another example of an emotional viewfinder at work? Have you heard the one about the little girl who prayed for a pony? One day she opened the door to her bedroom and was greeted with a room full of sh#@*!t well over her head. She squealed with delight. *"There's a pony in here somewhere!"*

There's a viewfinder that is working! Practice using yours through this full moon with any event—especially any results you have gotten from the first cycle. And don't forget to write them down. **Now get out there and find your pony!**

see you near the WaNiNG mOOn!

aWaReNeSS*musingsdooDLeSphotosFuN*

mORemusingsdooDLeSphotosFuN

mORe*musings*dooDLeS*photos*FuN

AWARENESS: *waning*...

This cycle's waning moon starts on _____

"To have faith is to trust yourself to the water.
When you swim you don't grab hold of the water, because if you do
you will sink and drown. Instead you relax, and float."
– Alan Watts –

So, how do we adjust our viewfinders for this releasing phase of the moon? I know! Let's look at the power of choice. Now that you are so adept with your viewfinder, you can examine all the angles and compositions you have captured and decide which angles will be more likely to produce a masterpiece and which ones you need to toss into the doodle drawer. You are not at the mercy of circumstances. You get to choose how you wish to experience the art of living your life.

One of the greatest gifts I received from the events recorded in *Bernadette's Pages*—that still holds true today—was the acute awareness of how my experience was determined by the way I cast my viewfinder. Was I the victim? The victimizer? Or neither? Whether viewing my relationship with God, myself, my husband, my creative passions, my career (or lack thereof), my spirituality, or simply ways that I could play, I got to choose how I wanted to see what was happening around me. When I looked at it as a classroom, it became a phenomenal experience that answered many prayers.

That one simple shift in perception determined the nature of my personal reality. That one simple shift—note I say simple, not easy—shaped the life I have today. I would not go back and change a thing. Guess you could say I found my pony.

WANING **moon***dance* STEPS•••

Now you are going to put your viewfinder expertise to the test.

••• List three events—or results—that you feel challenged by and would like to see differently. With viewfinder in mind, ask yourself these two questions:

1. What would this look like if love were present?
The beauty of love is that it is always present. If it is not immediately obvious in the circumstances outside you, then look for it within.

2. How would this feel if I chose love instead of fear?
Identify your fear then look for love to help you release it.

Remember...

Sometimes love looks like, "No, not yet." Or, "No, not this way."

Sometimes love looks like, "Why settle for good enough when, with a little more time, you can have the very best."

And sometimes love looks like a shovel.

see you at the WaXiNG mOOn when you'll revisit the power of iNTeNTioN!

aWaReNeSS*musingsdooDLeSphotos*FuN

aWaReNeSS*musings*dooDLeS*photos*FuN

mORemusingsdooDLeSphotosFuN

mORemusingsdooDLeSphotosFuN

INTENTION: *waxing*•••

"If you do not play your part, your part will go unplayed."
– Matthew Kelly –

Doodle or masterpiece? What are you creating?

"Applying intention without awareness is like a using a road map with no destination in mind. We find ourselves traveling to a lot of places that we may not want to visit—unless it was our intention to meander. If intention enlists so much power when it meets with the law of attraction wouldn't we like to know where we are going? (Or at least know how we got there if it's not to our liking?)" – Part One: Intention: Waxing

In the last moon cycle, you used a viewfinder to see your world through the artist's eyes. In doing so, you may have glimpsed—or felt the stirrings of—a masterpiece. Don't toss that viewfinder just yet because now, like the artist, you are going to begin the process of choosing the medium and materials that best support your vision—and that viewfinder will help you focus.

What will breathe life into your masterpiece? Into the art of living your best life? It is time to inventory what you already have in your "studio" and what you need to shop for. Sorting through what you have may inspire you to think outside the box. Maybe you will even discover a new purpose or a unique twist for something old. (An approach that turns many a doodle into a masterpiece, by the way.) Shopping for what you don't have may take you around the world—well out of your comfort zone. Or perhaps you will be surprised to find that what you need is available right in your own backyard.

As the moon waxes, the power of intention grows. Embrace this visioning process. Focus on your intentions and allow the light of awareness to reveal their true nature.

WAXING **moon** *dance* STEPS···

● ● ●   Make a list of what you would like to use to "paint your masterpiece." (Hint. These are your intentions.)

Note what you may already have and what you still need to "materialize." (You may want to review part one's waxing and full moon lists for intention.)

● ● ●   Now, you are going to put all those magazines you've been stacking up to good use. (You know. The ones you are going to read someday?) Clip images, words, and phrases that represent or support what you have on your list and put them in an empty cereal box. Yes. You read that right.

● ● ●   Start each day with your cereal box of champion-ideas. Dump your clippings out of the box and into a bowl. Shuffle them around. Lay them before you. Look at them through your viewfinder. Go ahead. Play with your food! Let your subconscious energize them. (I know some of you like to eat cereal at night so, if evenings work better for you, go for it.)

Add to your clippings between now and the full moon. You can't help but smile, carrying that cereal box around. And a smile invites wonderful energy to this process.

may your cereal box be overflowing with magical crackles and pops! See you at the FuLL mOOn.

iNTeNTioN*musings*dooDLeS*photos*FuN

mORemusingsdooDLeSphotosFuN

INTENTION: *full* ...

This cycle's full moon starts on _____

*"Every decision you make—every decision—is not a decision about what to do.
It's a decision about Who You Are. When you understand this, everything changes.
You begin to see life in a new way. All events, occurrences, and situations
turn into opportunities to do what you came here to do."*
– Neale Donald Walsch –

This full moon comes with one simple prompt: I hope your box of champion-ideas
is full of images that prime your creative juices and that you have been able to
spend a little bit of time "seeing" them through your viewfinder.

Now, consider what these images would represent to you without peace. Do not
assume peace is a given in this dualistic world of cereal box images. You have
to choose peace—just as you did any of those images that found their way into
your box.

A powerful thought for a powerful moon. How would any of these intentions feel
were they not partnered with peace?

FULL **moon***dance* STEPS•••

• • • Dump the images out of your box. Pick one to work with.

Using your emotional viewfinder, ask yourself if this image represents an intention framed by fear or lack. If so, find the loving view. State that you wish to experience peace. If you can't "get there" then go to the next image and repeat the process. Find the loving view. Ask for peace.

> *"... will you know what, in your experience, is worth the attention and so the intention that you give? It is intentions that create your life experience. Where would misdirected or misunderstood intentions place your life? ... stop looking at what you don't have, or you will create even more. Consider the gift of what it is you can see and use it ..."*
>
> *– Spirit Dialog, Bernadette's Pages*

<u>*Intentions can serve love or fear.*</u> Read that twice! If these intentions serve love, they will strengthen your trust in The Divine and open the door to peace. If they serve fear, they will reinforce a belief in the need to control, manipulate, or campaign for what you wish to experience.

• • • Now clip images that encourage a feeling of peace and tranquility and add them to your box. This will visually strengthen your intention for peace.

Go about this lightly. And remember to listen for the magical crackles and pops.

see you near the WaNiNG mOOn!

iNTeNTioN*musingsdooDLeSphotos*FuN

mORemusingsdooDLeSphotosFuN

INTENTION: *waning*•••

"Thirty spokes are made ... one by holes in a hub
By vacancies joining them for a wheel's use;
The use of clay in molding pitchers
Comes from the hollow of its absence;
Doors, windows in a house,
Are used for their emptiness:
Thus we are helped by what is not
To use what is."
– Lao Tzu, The Way of Life –

Ah, it is the releasing phase of the moon. Inhale as deeply as you can and hold it. Exhale slowly and allow yourself to feel the peace of release.

By now, you have a cereal box full of fun and exciting clippings of images that represent your best intentions, as well as images that represent peace. And, if you did your moondancing steps from the full moon, you also have a good idea of what you are going to release with this waning moon; any intention that is not yet partnered with a desire for peace. Any intention fueled by lack and limitation. Or, to put it another way, you are going to let go of the fear and re-frame your intention with love.

This moon supports the release of misguided beliefs—beliefs that invite stress and uncertainty into your life.

When fueled by fear, even the best of intentions can lead to places you may not want to go. Again, this Spirit scribe reminds us to pause and consider:

> *"It is intentions that create your life experience. Where would misdirected or misunderstood intentions place your life?"*

Misdirected and misunderstood intentions led me to places I do not care to revisit. How 'bout you?

WANING **moon***dance* STEPS•••

Using your emotional viewfinder, look at each of your clippings and ask yourself two questions:

1. What does this feel like in the presence of Peace?

2. What does this look like in the presence of Love?

Remove any intention (clipping) not yet ready to partner with love and your desire for peace. Don't judge this. Be gentle. Put it in an envelope and place it in the care of The Divine. When the time is right for it to manifest in love and not fear, you will get back to it. Be grateful for this awareness. You just saved yourself a lot of heartache. Embrace the process, however long it takes, and remember...

> *"Patience is natural to those who trust." – A Course In Miracles*

During the next moon phase we will toss a little Action and Feng Shui into the pot.

see you for some **aCTioN** at the **WaXiNG mOOn!**

iNTeNTion *musings* dooDLeS *photos* FuN

or paste your "CaRe oF THe DiViNe" envelope here.

iNTeNtion*musingsdooDLeSphotos*FuN

mORemusingsdooDLeSphotosFuN

mORemusingsdooDLeSphotosFuN

ACTION: *waxing*•••

This cycle's waxing moon starts on _____

"Even God can't steer a parked car."
"A road map never took anyone anywhere."

These two quotes were posted at eye level in my workspace years ago—back in my other life. I wish I could give proper credits to their source but that information has been long forgotten. (An internet search shows many who claim them. The earliest credit I found was a 1998 Unity article, which would have been around the time of that other life.)

I can, however, give credit and extend gratitude to Source. God knows why these quotes were so important to me. My life at that time screamed for action. Action that required a leap of faith that came in the form of quitting a job and career that I had been tied to for over fifteen years. (Even though I had no idea what I was going to be when I grew up. That information had not yet been revealed.)

God also knows why I have never forgotten these quotes. See, I am one of those Aquarians who loves to float around in the clouds dreaming up things not yet manifest in this world. When I get on a creative high I see possibilities—amazing possibilities. All that cloud hopping is exactly why the coaching work I do through MuseFusions is so perfect for me. Working with others to create a nurturing and safe place within their home keeps me grounded and gives me a way to seed the amazing possibilities I see into the present moment for those around me.

This is why I love inviting Feng Shui into the action part of this formula because Feng Shui reminds you that ideas without action are just that. Ideas. What a great way to put your car in drive, and see where that map you are holding will lead you!

WAXING **moon** *dance* STEPS•••

Here we are at the waxing moon with fresh energy and new ideas.

<u>Back to your cereal box!</u> Dump your clippings out and lay them before you. Shuffle them around. Look at them through your viewfinder and pick a clipping that represents an intention that you feel ready to work with.

••• Make a list of three actions that you could take right now to support that intention. (Join a club. Subscribe to a periodical. Sign up for a class. Make a phone call.)

Pick one action and *take it before the moon is full.*

Anchor that action in with one of these Feng Shui adjustment that address the center of your house; the solar plexus of your home.

••• Place a vase or pot of yellow chrysanthemums as close to your home's center as you can. If a closet or narrow hallway occupies the center of your home, place the chrysanthemums in the center of a kitchen or dining room table. This will provide you with a visual that reminds you to stay grounded as you take the action to support your intention. (Use yellow daisies if no mums are available.)

••• Really hate yellow? Then use red mums or a large red candle. In Feng Shui, red introduces the fire element. Fire makes earth and so represents the constructive cycling of chi.

Side Note: In Feng Shui, the center is supported by the earth element—the ground on which you stand. Yellow enhances earth energy. Yellow also encourages mental clarity. Focus in this area enhances your ability to remain centered and connected to what sustains you through life's transitions. Even good stuff can create chaos if you are not grounded and centered. (Just ask any actor in Hollywood who has made it big and lost site of their soul in the shuffle. Isn't it curious that the movie industry is centered in an earthquake zone where the earth is constantly shifting?)

Double Side Note: If the center of your home is cluttered, guess what you will be doing at the waning moon? For now, just do your best to make the Feng Shui adjustments suggested here.

see you near the FuLL mOOn!

paste "YeLLoW sTuFF" or an envelope here.

aCTioN*musings*dooDLeS*photos*FuN

mOREmusingsdooDLeSphotosFuN

mOREmusingsdooDLeSphotosFuN

ACTION: *full* •••

This cycle's full moon starts on _____

*"You cannot see the invisible. Yet if you see its effects
you know it must be there. By perceiving what it does, you recognize its being.
And by what it does, you learn what it is. You cannot see your strengths,
but you gain confidence in their existence as they enable you to act.
And the results of your actions you can see.*

*What you cannot see becomes real to you only through the witnesses
that speak for It. For you can be aware of what you cannot see,
and It can become compellingly real to you as Its Presence
becomes manifest through you."*
– A Course in Miracle: Chapter 12, Looking Within –

One of the things I love about Feng Shui is that it provides you with actions that help to bridge the seen with the unseen. When you take these "prescribed" actions and relate to what you witness, you get to discover more about the nature of your reality.

Chi is a word used in Feng Shui to describe energy or life force. Think of chi as electricity. You cannot see electricity in your home, but you witness its effects whenever you flip a switch. Until you flip a switch, electricity exists for you as potential. Potential that can fry you or illuminate you, depending on your action. Like electricity, you cannot see chi but you can see its effects.

Feng Shui shows you where the chi switches are. Action (flipping those switches), coupled with awareness and intention, can enlighten you as potential manifests into form. Finding and flipping those switches that support you—body, mind, and spirit—is what this moondance is all about.

"You cannot see your strengths, but you gain confidence in their existence as they enable you to act."

FULL **moon***dance* STEPS•••

Have you taken that one action you decided on?

Are you enjoying your yellow—or red—chrysanthemums?

Are you ready to light up the sky with your dreams?

• • • Step out tonight and look at the moon. And while you do, take a deep breath. As you exhale, let your breath reach out and connect with the unseen. Feel the synergy, created by moondancers manifesting all around the world, reaching out to support you as you move toward your dream. On your next deep breath and exhale, send out your gratitude and support.

Feel the chi—the life force of this evening gently lifting away the day's concerns. Physically reach up and out. Stretch as far as you comfortably can. As you do, extend gratitude to all the unseen support that flows through your life—then give yourself a great big hug. As a matter of fact, how about a group hug?

see you near the WaNiNG mOOn!

aCTioN*musings*dooDLeS*photos*FuN

mORe*musings*dooDLe*Sphotos*FuN

ACTION: *waning*•••

This cycle's waning moon starts on _____

"Many a false step is made standing still."
– Chinese Proverb –

During the intention phase of the waning moon (part two), you were encouraged to release any misguided beliefs that invited stress and uncertainty into your life. And you were reminded that, when fueled by fear, even the best of intentions lead to places you might not want to go. That's because fear blocks energy, and blocked energy creates the need for detours and distractions.

During the action phase of this waxing moon and full moon, you were encouraged to make one Feng Shui adjustment and take one positive action step toward manifesting your intention. The Feng Shui application during this waning moon will be a little different. You will support your awareness and intention by what you remove.

This is a powerful time to sort and purge. Physical purging is a wonderful way to get the blocked energy moving in any area of your life. If you combine this purging action with awareness and intention, you focus the energy in a more direct and efficient way. No need for detours or distractions here unless they serve your very best interest!

WANING **moon***dance* STEPS•••

Ah, the releasing phase of the moon. Inhale as deeply as you can and hold it. Exhale slowly and allow yourself to feel the release.

It is time to start clearing any clutter that is hanging around the center of your home. Remember, in Feng Shui, the center represents earth energy—the ground on which you stand. An orderly center supports your ability to focus and balance. Clutter in the center supports chaos and constricts flow.

••• What is in the center of your home? Is it a closet? A room? A hallway?

••• What kind of shape is it in? Is it in need of sorting? Is it in need of purging? Organize everything that still serves you, in an orderly and easily accessible fashion. Let go of anything that is broken or no longer serves you. (If the broken object needs fixing then get it fixed or pass it on.)

Don't have any clutter in the center of your home? Good for you! There is no action you need to take. You have done it with the chrysanthemums. Sit back and enjoy them.

However—wink-wink—you could find another area that is in need of some purging. Go through that junk drawer or the back of your bedroom closet. Or go ahead and purge those old files at the office.

All sorting and purging is to be done mindfully, of course. Remember, it is not how much you do but how mindfully you do it!

see you at the WaXiNG mOOn where you refocus on ReSuLTS!

aCTioN*musings*dooDLeS*photos*FuN

mOREmusingsdooDLeSphotosFuN

RESULTS: *waxing...*

> *"When one door closes another door opens.*
> *But sometimes it is hell in the hallway."*
> *– Anonymous –*

Okay. A déjà vu warning comes with this moon message. Forgive me. I am not lazy. (Well, maybe sometimes—but not without good reason.) This slightly edited message, from Part One's waxing moon results, bears repeating.

Why is this message so important? The quote above offers a clue. I am willing to bet that you know more than a little bit about hanging out in that hallway. This waxing moon invites a positive shift in your perception should you find yourself waiting for the other door to open.

> *And they lived happily ever after. The end?... In the debatable glory of the afterglow, this ain't Venus! We are still very much on this planet. The mountains are beautiful to look at from a distance and open to an inspiring panorama from their crest. Climbing them, however, invites an entirely different view. In that climb, there are days when happily-ever-after screams for chucking this relationship into the recycling bin, when the siren voices discredit every conquered peak, every incredible vista shared, and threaten to send us dashing to the rocks below.*
>
> *Their wails echo, "You prayed for this? What were you thinking? You'll never make it!"*
>
> *– Bernadette's Pages: An Intimate Crossroad*

Without further ado, begin Déjà vu here:

Results are results. Or are they? This is where many of us can get lost. Which is why I want you to think of a result as a point on a map. How much does that point tell you about all there is to experience in Hollywood, California? That point encompasses a lot of territory. But what does that point define? If you live in Hollywood, it defines everything. If you do not, it defines nothing truly usable as a personal experience. (Is this coming back to you now? If you are leafing back to check; Yes, I did take you to Sante Fe, New Mexico the first time around. Thought you could use a change of scenery.)

When working a formula like this, results are not the destination. They are still a part of the journey. You do not take up permanent residence with a result—or a dot on the map.

This is the part of the formula where you pay attention, like you would if you were driving into Hollywood for the first time. Results (the arrival zone) now call for more awareness (watch those street signs), clarified intention (decide what you want to see and do in this new terrain), and fine-tuned action (turn right at the big blue billboard).

End Déjà vu here.

Is your destination point the same as it was when you first started working with this formula? Are you fine-tuning your results while getting to know the neighborhood? Are you working on reroutes because new discoveries about yourself dictate different scenery? Are you celebrating in the arrival zone? Or ... did you get stuck in the hallway at the visitor's welcome center?

Whatever your deal is during this waxing moon, don't stop dancing. You know the steps. You've got some great muscle built up here and you get to decide how you want to use it.

WAXING **moon***dance* STEPS•••

As the moon gains in fullness, look for synchronicities—again. They point the way and affirm your path. Pay attention to song verses, billboards and 18-wheelers, books and movies, unexpected offers and new introductions. (Is this step starting to sound familiar?) Yep. All those signpost-results that help fine-tune your focus— or offer a playful patience should you find yourself waiting in the hallway.

Synchronicity Journal: Did your synchronicity journal get buried? Well, pull it back out and reacquaint yourself. And remember, it's not just for present synchronicities—past or present count for this journal.

In case you didn't do this the first time, here's a refresher: This can be a small journal or tablet—easily carried in your purse or pocket—in which you write one synchronicity per page. This format allows you to recapture each moment at a glance and helps to beef up your faith muscle when divine order calls for a little more time and patience than you were planning to expend. It also helps you hone your intuition. And you can occupy yourself with this litany-list of synchronicities when there seems to be a "hush" in that hallway.

see you near the FuLL mOOn!

"WHaTNoTs ZoNe" for treasure envelope, or whatever you like!

ReSuLTS*musingsdoo*DLeS*photos*FuN

RESULTS: *full* •••

This cycle's full moon starts on _____

> *"Cherish the process that led you, embraced you, cajoled you, prodded you,*
> *and got you from there to this moment, NOW.*
> *Remember when you were King of the Mountain and Queen of the Hula Hoop?*
> *The mountains may be larger now and the hula hoops smaller but*
> *the magic still lies within the process of discovering YOU."*
>
> *– ME –*

There was a song that played on the radio a number of years ago. It was performed by a group from Germany called Dancing Fantasy and entitled *Walk of Life*.

Something about this song resonated so strongly with me that, whenever it played, I stopped what I was doing to "take it in." And, in doing so, would find myself lost in a daydream that never failed to lift my spirit. I would see myself dancing alone in the center of a large circular clearing deep within a forest—happily twirling about like a leaf carried on a gentle breeze.

One day a question popped into my head. What would happen if I thought of people I knew who were troubled or challenged and "invited" them to join me in this imaginary dance? And what if, no matter where they were or what they were doing in the "real world," they found their day lighter, their spirit brighter because of it?

At first, just a few joined me. Some came to the clearing and hopped right into the rhythm of the dance. Others timidly lingered on the edge, only to take a rain check for a later date.

It was not long before I found myself moved to buy *Walk of Life* so I could choose when I wanted to experience this dancing fantasy. I learned to let go of any need to control the visual, as it was not unusual for my little daydream to take on a life of its own. Sometimes people from the past showed up, or people that I needed to do healing and forgiveness work with. Often, by the time the tune ended, countless twirling bodies and bobbing heads would surround me. Many of whom I did not know. Friends of friends of friends. Dancers and music-makers sharing the joy of a communal experience.

This fantasy remained a happy pick-me-up for a few years before life got busy with the distraction of two cross-country moves. Between packing and unpacking, settling and unsettling, I did not think to listen to it. The path to my magical forest clearing soon lay hidden beneath overgrown brush and fallen leaves.

I was settling in from one of these moves when I met a woman with whom I felt an instant connection. She hired me to come to her home to do a little Feng Shui and to help organize her "whimsy room." (She was a writer in the throws of writing a novel and in need of a sanctuary that would sustain and inspire her.)

Her home was nestled far off the main road where she and her husband owned a fairly large acreage of forest. As our friendship deepened, she shared a dream that was about to become a reality for her. She had created a labyrinth, tucked away in the forest by her home, and was in the process of putting the finishing touches on it. She had plans for a special labyrinth walk—a ceremony that would share her vision for peace and joy with many.

One afternoon, just prior to this event, she invited me to walk it with her. To feel its power. Leaves and twigs crunched under our feet as she led me into the woods. The site she had chosen was impressive and substantial. As we silently spiraled our way into the center of her labyrinth, a mystical stillness settled into everything around us. The land felt sacred. The air felt charged. When we finished our meditative walk, we sat and talked about her plans for the ceremony. She asked if I would lead the labyrinth procession in a dance. Honored, I said yes.

Her vision manifested into an amazing event. Several hundred people, invited from all walks of life and religious practices, were there. Her writing coach facilitated it. A Taoist monk blessed it. A Baptist minister brought his church choir to sing *Amazing Grace* for it.

A ceremonial drummer provided the beat for our symbolic "walk of life" as I led her guests, in dance, into the labyrinth's center and out. I was halfway in before I "came to" and realized that all the smiling faces and twirling bodies around me were strangely reminiscent of my own dancing fantasy. A fantasy that took on a life of its own in a way that I could never have imagined—and continues to amaze me to this day!

FULL **moon** *dance* STEPS•••

I invite you to take a moment to consider the application of awareness, intention, and action in my story.

AWARENESS: I was aware of the song's impact on me and mindfully chose to relax and "take it in."

INTENTION: I anchored the joyful feelings that it gave me with an intention to share it.

ACTION: I took the action to buy the CD and play it with the same awareness and intention that drew me to it.

RESULTS: My results were always that I felt better afterward. The labyrinth walk was a miraculous bonus. An unanticipated extra that now serves to reinforce this amazing process.

Remember, a synchronicity may precede a desired result, guiding you in a particular direction. Or it may BE the result, revealing itself to you in an extraordinary manner to capture your attention. Either way, looking for synchronicities is a fun way to fine-tune when working with this formula.

As you enjoy the full moon, continue to notice, recall, and record synchronicities in your journal. Or decorate some of your pages with doodles, photos, and magazine clippings to visually strengthen a particular synchronicity. Have fun with it!

see you near the WaNiNG mOOn!

ReSuLTS*musings*dooDLeS*photos*Fun

mORemusingsdooDLeSphotosFuN

mORemusingsdooDLeSphotosFun

RESULTS: *waning...*

This cycle's waning moon starts on _____

"Don't get good at what you don't want to be doing."
– Anonymous –

As moondancing fate would have it, though I looked high and low, on the dark side of the moon and bright, I could not find any copy for this final moondancing cycle from the original series. It seems to have waned out of existence. The muses apparently intended that I write something new to take us out on the last chord because I am usually very good at keeping my writing resources organized, as writing is "what I DO want to be doing." Hmmm. No coincidences, right?

With this waning moon, I find myself thinking about the divine relationship between noun and verb found in the word resource. What, you say? Resource is not a verb? Well, are you up for a little waning moon wordplay? Pulling out my dictionary now.

> **re • source** *noun.* [Old French, *re-*, again + *sourdre*, spring up]
> 1. something that lies ready for use or can be drawn upon for aid.
> 2. wealth; assets

Hmmm. You might be right but, at the moment, I am feeling a little resourceful— *adjective.* able to deal effectively with problems—so shall we proceed?

Lets break it down and look at re.

> **re-** [French or Latin] *a prefix meaning;* 1. back 2. again; anew

Adjust. Readjust. Affirm. Reaffirm. Align. Realign. Assess. Reassess. Awaken. Reawaken... Born. Reborn. Build. Rebuild... Check. Recheck. Cover. Re-cover... (Yes, there's supposed to be a hyphen—just checking to see if you are reading or scanning.)

What a hard working prefix re is. With one hundred and six RE-words listed in my old 1983 Webster paperback, how can there not be verb potential for resource in here somewhere?

Now lets look at source.

> **source** *noun.* [Latin, *surgere,* to rise]   1. a spring, etc. from which a stream arises   2. place of origin; prime cause   3. a person, book, etc. that provides information

Well, source may be a noun but there is a lot of activity surrounding it. Stuff has to happen for something to be a source. Reread all these definitions, resourcefully, and you might see where I am going with this and why resource makes a perfect word for our final dance because with RE+SOURCE+RESULTS there is no grand finale—only grand re-creations.

So, here's resource—when noun meets verb—from Bernadette's dictionary.

> **re • SOURCE** *verb. noun.* [Divine]   1. when action collaborates with Source to expand one's capability to be part of the evolutionary flow of creation   2. the ongoing activity under which the universe grows   3. the personal engagement with Source to bring about a continued desire to re

When you re-source with SOURCE you re-source your resources to "rise up again to meet prime cause anew" so that you can revise, repurpose or recycle your results—thus you will never be stuck residing or re-siding with them.

What a perfect waning moon contemplation this is, eh?

WANING **moon** *dance* STEPS•••

In this dance with the moon, your resources led you to results. In contemplating whether they hit or missed the mark you get to decide whether your results offer resources (noun) you can use—or if you wish to re-Source (verb) those resources.

I want you to keep the wordplay going while the moon wanes to reinforce your understanding that nothing is permanent and that the best results offer continued opportunities to transmute and fine-tune your life—and how you wish to experience it.

●●● Make a re-word gratitude list. Yes. Just singular re-words that you are grateful for. As you feel the gratitude grow, a surge of concentrated energy will be yours to tap into for any reSOURCE-FULLness you wish to expand upon. (Go ahead and revisit the dictionary and pluck out the ones you relate to. Here are a few to get you started.)

Rewind. Rekindle. Reacquaint. Reposition. Republish. Reheat. Remarry...

●●● Scramble a re-word in an affirmation sentence by messing with re-noun-verb usage. (Use your dictionary of experience. Perhaps you will uncover words and meanings waiting to be birthed.) Here are a few examples.

When someone cuts me down, I always remember to re-member, not dismember, my self.

Repetition helps me to re-petition my mind with the things that are important.

More recreation for me invites re-creation of me.

●●● Replay times in your life where you benefited from a re-word transition. Choose words from your gratitude list and see what pops up. Write down your thoughts and impressions of the experience. You may find that some re-word

experiences surfaced after events you were not, at the time, grateful for but— because they transitioned with a re—transmuted to a positive. (Like marrying, divorcing, and remarrying.)

ReSuLTSmusingsdooDLeSphotosFuN

mORe*musings*dooDLeS*photos*FuN

mOREmusingsdooDLeSphotosFuN

IN *closing*, SHINE *on!*

I know. It's hard to believe that eight moon cycles have passed since we first cued the music and you started turning these pages. Pages that I hope are filled with messy notes and doodles and clippings that will keep you humming and dancing with delight.

This series is now complete but the moon shines on. I hope that our time spent together, dancing under the moonlight, continues to inspire you to use the moon and this formula whenever you feel a need to supercharge any aspect of your life. You now know what a little awareness, intention, and action can do.

No doubt new directions have come into focus for many of you. I'm always excited to hear stories about moondancing discoveries and synchronicities so feel free to share them with me. The *about the author* page in the back of this book will link you to the places where you'll likely catch me dancing. And, if you are one of the creative folk or group of creative folks that have joined in dance, I would love to hear about—and see—your creations. Subscribe to my *Musings from the Messy Room* blog so you will not miss notifications about when and where to share your creative inspirations and stories.

Whether you are dancing solo or with a group, the moon we see is the same, my friend. So lets keep tapping into that wonderful moon energy and share our own light with the world so that others might know the joy of the dance.

sHiNe oN, LoVeLY mOOnDaNCeRs!

acKNoWLeDGeMeNTs

With happy feet and heartfelt humming, I shower my gratitude and love...

To my precious family and friends who share this dance with me, even when the music gets faint. I wouldn't be dancing today without you in my heart.

To those who entered my life as clients, honored me with their trust, and are now friends who I get to break out in dance with when life sees fit to merge our moons. You make this the best "too good to be a real job" in the world.

To the online family that continues to grow and enrich my life with the kind of inspired sharing that extends this ballroom, one continent at a time, and exponentially multiplies the possibilities for happy dancing. What marvelous traveling companions you are.

To my angels, divine guides, delightful muses, and departed beloveds who inspire me from the realm of the unseen-but-oh-so-felt. With you I get to dance with wings on my feet.

To God, my Divine Source and best Creative Collaborator, who gifts me with more creative ideas than I could ever hope to birth into this world. You never diminish or dismiss any project-twist I come up with, and always guide me to re-Source the resources that lead me home to You—dancing.

aBouT THe auTHoR

"Let the beauty of what you love be what you do." – Rumi

Bernadette Rose Smith is an artist and writer, and the resident muse of MuseFusions; the umbrella under which she inspires, assists, and coaches others while engaging in all the activities that she loves to share. (Well, most all.) As a muse, she offers an eclectic mix of inspiration for heart, home, and lifestyle support designed to stir, excite, and release the energy needed to sustain more of what makes folks smile—no matter what their dance.

"LiFe is meSSy. bE YOU aNYway."– bRs

For information on all the heart and home coaching services Bernadette offers or to keep up with her seminar and workshop schedule, visit her website at musefusions.com.

If you prefer to come in through the back door to peek in on her latest projects-in-process, art, and messy musings, hop over to her blog, *Musings from the Messy Room*, at enlightenedink.com/blog. (But don't expect her to clean up.)

Bernadette currently enjoys life in the greater Atlanta area while frequently breaking out in dance with clients, friends, family, and her furry meow-muses.

awareness • intention • action • results •

a SPeCiaL $1.99 *offer*

"Reading theses pages will feel more like eavesdropping, at first.
With the edginess that comes when you stumble within earshot of what
you recognize immediately is a very private conversation..."

"I love you." Three simple words.

"There's someone else." Three simple words.

Ever fall in love? Ever fall out? In the roundabout from "I do" to "I don't" to "Now what," this book shares a love story of a different kind.

If you are struggling with finding forgiveness after a betrayal—or just curious to read the story about how one woman managed to manifest a beautiful mess under duress—take advantage of this special offer for Moondancers.

To order your $1.99 copy of *Bernadette's Pages: An Intimate Crossroad* ...
go to the link below. Find out more about the book and its unique format, read reviews, and order your $1.99 copy today.

> • **Your Special $1.99 Moondancing Link** •
>
> ## http:// enlightenedink.com/special-199-offer

"...the insightful and deeply personal account of an incredible journey through
love, loss, and self-discovery...vividly written and inherently wise...
Bernadette's Pages is very strongly recommended reading..."
–The Midwest Book Review

* $1.99 offer can be accessed through this link only.   ** Shipping not included in this price

moon *dancing*

delight in the dance that is your

134

Made in the USA
Las Vegas, NV
24 January 2023

66203623R00083